World Religions and Beliefs

THE Birth OF Christianity

World Religions and Beliefs

THE Birth OF Christianity

Don Nardo

MORGAN REYNOLDS
PUBLISHING

Greensboro, North Carolina

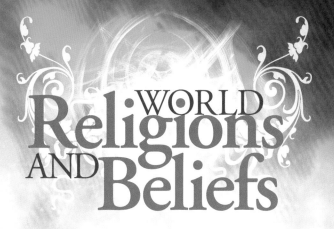

WORLD
Religions
AND Beliefs

Founders of Faiths

Mystics and Psychics

The Birth of Christianity

The Birth of Islam

World Religions and Beliefs: The Birth of Christianity

Copyright © 2012 by Morgan Reynolds Publishing

Library of Congress Cataloging-in-Publication Data

Nardo, Don, 1947-
The birth of Christianity / by Don Nardo.
   p. cm.
Includes bibliographical references.
ISBN 978-1-59935-145-2
1. Church history--Primitive and early church, ca. 30-600--Juvenile
literature. I. Title.
BR162.3.N37 2011
270.1--dc22

                                        2010038443

Printed in the United States of America
First Edition

Herdsmen worshiping the baby Jesus, in a painting by Italian Renaissance artist Giorgio Barbarelli da Castelfranco.

Contents

Chapter

1

Greeks, Romans, and Jews

With more than 2 billion people belonging to thousands of separate denominations, Christianity is the world's largest religion. However, at first Christianity was not even a separate faith. The earliest Christians made up a tiny and unassuming sect of Judaism, the faith of the Jews that was rooted in ancient Palestine. "The first Christians were first-century [AD] Jews," points out theologian Justo González, "and it was as such that they heard and received the [Christian] message." After Jesus of Nazareth, the man who had inspired them, died in the early 30s CE, the faith experienced enormous growth. Initially Jesus's followers spread their message among fellow Jews, but eventually they began welcoming Gentiles (non-Jews) into the fold and not long after that Christianity broke away from Judaism.

Early Christians were unpopular among their fellow citizens of the Roman Empire, which spanned the entire Mediterranean region. Many Romans mistrusted, discriminated against, and persecuted Christians. Yet in the face of antagonism and abuse, the faith endured. Christians gradually gained acceptance and respectability, and by the late 300s the faith had swept through Roman society to become the Empire's most prevalent and influential religion.

The Roman context in which Christianity developed was a melting pot of ethnic, social, political, and religious ideas and customs—cultural forces that left a distinctive and lasting imprint on the faith in its formative years. Of these forces, Jewish culture had the greatest influence. Jewish spiritual practices and ethics served as prototypes for early Christians, and Jewish scriptures—the Old Testament—came to constitute more than half of the Christian Bible. González affirms the importance of the Roman-Jewish context in Christianity's development, stating that, "in order to understand the history of Christianity in its early centuries [one] must begin by looking at the world in which it evolved."

The Greco-Roman World

Christianity emerged at a time when Rome dominated much of the known world. In the three centuries preceding Jesus's birth, the Romans had first gained power over the Italian peninsula and then defeated the maritime empire of Carthage, centered in North Africa. These victories gave Rome control of the western portion of the Mediterranean sphere. The Romans next

Opposite Page: Carthage under siege by the Roman army, as depicted in this hand-colored reproduction of a nineteenth-century illustration

turned eastward and conquered Greece and the Greek-ruled lands. These included the large monarchies in Egypt and the Middle East that had been founded in the fourth and third centuries BCE by the successors of Alexander the Great.

By adding these lands to its empire, Rome gained control of Palestine, where the Jewish kingdoms of Israel and Judah had once thrived. This territory collectively became the Roman province of Judea.

Like many other peoples the Romans had overrun, the Jews disliked being subject to Roman authority and yearned for independence.

Although Rome imposed its political will and laws on the peoples it conquered, often at sword-point, it also brought economic order, prosperity, and security to those regions. Trade flourished, new towns emerged, and some existing towns developed and expanded into bustling cities. To facilitate this growth, the Romans constructed an enormous system of roads that connected all corners of its Empire. These roads would later make it relatively easy for early Christians to spread their ideas and communities far and wide.

PRAISING ROME'S ACHIEVEMENTS

Writing in the second century BCE, Greek scholar Aelius Aristides praised Rome's economic prosperity:

The whole world speaks in unison [in] praying this Empire may last for all time. . . . Every place is full of gymnasia, fountains, gateways, temples, shops, and schools. . . . Gifts never stop flowing from you to the cities, [which] shine in radiance and beauty. . . . Only those outside your Empire are fit to be pitied for losing such blessings. . . . Greek and [non-Greek] can now readily go wherever they please with their property or without it. . . . You have surveyed the whole world, built bridges of all sorts across rivers, cut down mountains to make paths for chariots, filled the deserts with hostels, and civilized it all with system and order.

Although the Greeks, too, had been conquered by Rome, Greek culture retained significant influence throughout the Empire—much to Rome's annoyance. At the time the Greeks called themselves Hellenes, and the spread of Greek culture became known as Hellenism. J. R. Porter, late theologian and professor at the University of Exeter in England, explains Hellenism:

> Hellenism may be defined as the essentially Greek pattern of civilization that came to dominate the [Middle] East in the wake of the conquests of Alexander the Great

(ruled 332–323 BCE). It embraced language, lifestyle, education, economy, philosophy, and religion. Its general effect was to bring diverse existing societies within a common culture. For example, it encouraged "syncretism"—the equation of one god with another as forms of the same deity.

The Jewish king Herod the Great, who ruled from 37 to 4 BCE (the period in which Jesus was born), was a fervent disciple of Hellenism. He erected Greek-style cities and even pagan temples like those of the Greeks. His disrespect for Jewish traditions sowed as much, if not more, hatred amongst Jews as Rome's policies did, and Herod often caused trouble for both Jewish and Roman officials. Porter emphasizes that discontented Jews "view[ed] Hellenism as an alien culture and resented the wealth of its supporters." In his teachings, Jesus denounced the wealthy and corrupt elite, and Porter suggests that Jesus and his followers were openly critical of the lifestyle associated with Hellenism.

The Religious Scene

Before, during, and directly after Jesus's lifetime, a complex and dramatic religious system existed in the Roman Empire. Through the influence of Hellenism, most religions were polytheistic and most people believed that the gods of all religions were equally valid and worthy—notions that contradicted the Jewish belief in one supreme deity.

One of Judaism's chief competitors was Rome's traditional state religion. The Roman pantheon, or group of gods, consisted of Jupiter, its leader; his wife, Juno; the war-god Mars and war-goddess Minerva; the god of the arts and prophecy, Apollo; and other gods that mirrored those of the Greek pantheon. The Roman Jupiter was equivalent to the Greek Zeus; Minerva was the Roman version of the Greeks' Athena; and so on.

No less popular during this era were a number of so-called mystery cults, which had originated mostly in Greece and the Middle East. The term mystery referred to various secret initiations and sacred objects known only to the members of these faiths. The cult of Cybele, the "Great Mother," was particularly well known throughout the Empire, with its origins in Asia Minor (what is now Turkey). Cybele was a nature and fertility goddess whose priests performed self-castration in order to appease her. Another popular mystery cult was that of Mithras, from Persia (now Iran), whose adherents believed in treating all people with compassion and respect. Still another was the cult of Isis. Initially an Egyptian fertility goddess, many residents of the Roman Empire came to associate her with goodness and the purification of sin.

WORSHIPING ISIS

The second-century Roman novelist Apuleius penned this eyewitness account of some of Isis's worshipers during a religious festival:

[They] came surging along, men and women of every rank and age, gleaming with linen garments spotlessly white. The women had sprayed their hair with perfume [and] the men had shaved their heads completely, so that their bald pates shone. With their rattles of bronze, silver, and even gold, they made a shrill, tinkling sound [and] their leader held out a lamp gleaming with brilliant light. . . . [There was also] a golden boat-shaped vessel feeding quite a large flame from an opening at its centre.

Not surprisingly, the early Christians borrowed some of the ideas and images from the Empire's vast religious assemblage. At the center of Mithraism, for instance, was a narrative about the birth of a divine being in human form. It also featured a special meal of bread and wine, baptism, and the promise of life after death—ideas later adopted by Christians. British historian Charles Freeman explains the similarities between Christianity and the other religions in the Egyptian, Greek, and Roman worlds:

> Much of the imagery of the New Testament—light and darkness, faith compared to flourishing crops—is similar to that found in mystery religions. The 'facts' of Jesus's life were presented in a format which was not unique to him. . . . The promise of an afterlife for the initiated would have been commonplace to anyone who had contact with mystery religions. The development of the cult of Mary, the mother of Jesus, acquires a new richness when placed in parallel with the worship of other mother figures in these religions. . . . Many of the procedures of the mystery religions [became] important influences on Christian practice.

The Jews and the Messiah

Though apparent, such outside religious influences on early Christians were minor compared to those of Judaism. Because Christianity developed directly out of Judaism, Christians saw their god as one and the same with the Jewish god. The two faiths also shared an ethical tradition that, for example, stressed the constancy of family life and the importance of aiding the poor and sick. In addition, the Christian canon retained sacred Jewish writings, most importantly those that came to be called the Old Testament. Abraham, Moses, David, Solomon, and other ancient Hebrew prophets and kings became (and remain) heroic and sacred figures to Christians.

These were only some of the Jewish traditions and customs that shaped the lives of Jesus, those who knew him, and those who established the Christian faith after his death. Also instrumental were the several opposing factions and groups within the Jewish community. Each had its own approach to interpreting God's laws and to dealing with the Romans. The Zealots, for instance, the most radical Jewish group, advocated violence as a measure of resistance against their Roman occupiers. Noted English classicist Michael Grant summarizes the roles of more moderate Jewish groups:

> The Pharisees [were Judaism's] spiritual leaders and controlled the synagogues; the Sadducees . . . directed worship in the Temple at Jerusalem and collaborated with the Romans; the 'scribes' or doctors of the law [were] the experts on Judaism. . . ; and certain withdrawn, semi-hermit societies such as the [Essenes] of Qumran, on the Dead Sea . . . rejected what they regarded as the worldly errors and compromises of the other groups and [remained aloof and detached].

Although these Jewish sects disagreed on numerous issues, big and small, they all agreed on a few central beliefs. All worshiped the single deity of their ancestors; all revered the Jewish Scriptures; and all believed in the coming of the Messiah, or 'Anointed One.' The latter was a superhuman figure who, according to prophecies described in the Old Testament and other sacred writings, would rescue the Jews from their oppression.

In the words of A. N. Wilson, a British writer and biblical scholar: "The Messiah would come down from the clouds in the likeness of the Son of man in the Book of Daniel; he would establish a kingdom which was an everlasting kingdom, having first crushed [the Jews'] enemies under his feet; the old temple of Solomon would be restored in Jerusalem. [And] the Gentiles would worship the God of Israel."

No one was certain when the Messiah would arrive. Some, including the Essenes, the Jewish monks who lived at Qumran, near the Dead Sea, thought it might happen at any moment. Others said it was more likely to occur within a few generations or even longer. Christians, in contrast, believed that Jesus was the Messiah—that the prophecy had been fulfilled. And it was this belief that triggered Christianity's split from Judaism and its formation as a separate faith.

When asked why they thought Jesus was the Anointed One, the early Christians cited his life and deeds, which over time would inspire a great many others to faith.

Angels Announcing Christ's Birth to the Shepherds, a 1639 painting by Govert Flinck. On display at the Louvre Museum in Paris

A painting of the boy Jesus teaching at the temple

2

Jesus's Life and Teachings

The story of Jesus's life is contained in the biblical Gospels of Matthew, Mark, Luke, and John, which constitute the first four books of the New Testament. For most Christians, the Gospels serve as the primary source of information about Jesus's ministry, his closest followers (the Apostles, sometimes called his Disciples), the message he preached, and his death at the hands of the local authorities.

The accuracy of the Gospels is controversial. While many Christians testify that the books are true historical accounts, skeptics claim that the books were mostly fabricated. Most modern historians and biblical scholars fall somewhere between these extremes. They say these books weave valuable historical data with charismatic stories of miracles and other supernatural themes—elements of the Gospels that are difficult to prove or disprove and as such remain a matter of faith. Furthermore, the four narratives are not direct eyewitness accounts—they were written decades after Jesus's death by anonymous individuals who had never met him. (Their titles were given much later, in the second century.)

These scholars also point out that the writers of the Gospels aimed to demonstrate that Jesus was different and special—the one and only Messiah by virtue of the miracles he performed, the prophecies about him in the Old Testament, and his resurrection from the dead. Yet many other Jews of his time preached similarly about God and the imminent arrival of his holy Kingdom on Earth.

To verify Jesus's existence, modern historians refer not only to the Gospels, but also to non-Christian accounts from that time period. References to Jesus crop up in sources that range from biographies of Roman officials to histories penned by Jewish and Roman chroniclers.

Non-Christian Accounts of Jesus

If the Gospels were the only surviving records of Jesus, his existence would be dubious. However, most scholars accept his existence because of the survival of some non-Christian accounts that mention him. Most of these writings, says E. P. Sanders, a New Testament professor at Duke University, were "written by members of the very small elite class of the Roman Empire. To them, Jesus (if they heard of him at all) was merely a trouble-some rabble-rouser and magician in a small, backward part of the world."

The earliest of these accounts is that of the first-century Roman scholar Suetonius. Writing about Claudius, the Roman emperor who reigned from 41 to 54, he said: "Because the Jews at Rome caused continuous disturbances at the instigation of Chrestus, he [Claudius] expelled them from the city." This brief statement contains two revealing points. First, Chrestus is unar-guably a reference to Jesus Christ. *Christ* was not part of Jesus's name during his own lifetime, as many people today assume. It came from the Greek word *Christos,* which meant "Messiah." It was added to his given name, Jesus, by his followers only after his death.

And second, like most other Romans of that time, Suetonius made no distinction between Jews and Christians. This was no misnomer, since during Claudius's reign most Christians were still Jews.

A more fulsome mention of Jesus came from the great first-century Jewish historian Josephus. In 93, about sixty years after Jesus's death, he wrote:

> There was about this time, Jesus, a wise man, if it be lawful to call him a man, for he was a doer of wonder-ful works—a teacher of such men as receive the truth with pleasure. He drew over to him many of the Jews and many of the Gentiles. He was [the] Christ; and when [the Roman governor of Judea, Pontius] Pilate . . . had

condemned him to the cross, those that loved him at the first did not forsake him, for he appeared to them alive again the third day, as the divine prophets had foretold . . . and the tribe of the Christians, so named from him, are not extinct at this day.

His Life and Death

Accepting that Jesus was a real, historical figure, modern scholars have painstakingly constructed a partial overview of his life and death. The reason it remains partial is that ancient sources, including the Gospels, only make sparse references to his childhood and early adulthood. Except for a mention in the Gospels of his visit to Jerusalem with his parents as a young boy, all that has survived is some information about his birth, his travels as a preacher when he was in his early thirties, and his execution by the Romans.

Many biblical scholars contend that Jesus was born in about 5 or 4 BCE, the latter also being the year King Herod of Israel died. The Gregorian calendar that is today's international standard implies that his birth occurred in CE 1. However, this calendar is a modification of two different calendars: the Julian calendar, which was created in the first century CE and over the

Jesus (left) offering John the Baptist a drink of water, as portrayed in an oil painting by Bartolome Esteban Murillo.

The adoration of the
baby Jesus, by Mary
and the shepherds of
Bethlehem, as shown
in a painting by Guido
Reni. On display at St.
Martin's Charterhouse
in Naples, Italy

years shifted off track; and one created several centuries later by the Christian monk Exiguus. By the time Exiguus organized his calendar, the dates for events in Jesus's time were uncertain, leading Exiguus to make some educated guesses. His calculations turned out to be somewhat in error.

TRYING TO CALCULATE JESUS'S BIRTH YEAR

Modern specialists have determined that the dating of Jesus's birth by Dionysius Exiguus, the monk who made the Christian calendar, was off by a few years. After studying the Gospels, Exiguus concluded that Jesus was born in or about the year that King Herod passed away. However, the monk, working six centuries after the fact, was unable to pin down the exact year of Herod's death. Nor could he be sure of the date of the census mentioned in the Gospel of Luke, during which Jesus's mother, Mary, and her husband, Joseph, traveled to Judea to be counted. So Exiguus seems to have based his estimate on other events mentioned in the Gospels, including when John the Baptist began preaching (supposedly in the fifteenth year of the reign of the Roman emperor Tiberius). In any case, modern scholarship has rendered that estimate incorrect. The best guess today is that Jesus was born near the end of Herod's reign, possibly as early as 7 BCE, but more likely two or three years later.

In whatever year Jesus was born, most ancient sources affirm that shortly afterward Mary and Joseph settled in Nazareth, a town in Galilee, in northern Palestine. In the next substantial description of Jesus in these sources, he sets out to travel and preach at about the age of thirty. As for what he did as a child and young man, evidence is scant. One possibility, alluded to in the Gospels, is that he assisted Joseph, who was a carpenter. (Some scholars suggest that the two were stonemasons rather than carpenters.)

Another possibility is that Jesus spent part of his early adulthood studying the ideas of the Essenes. A few of Jesus's biographers speculate that he was himself a devout Essene, though there is little proof in support of this hypothesis. "A more plausible theory," writes J. R. Porter,

> is that Jesus (and John the Baptist) started out as Qumranites before leaving to embark on their own distinctive missions. Qumran was a closed body of initiates, similar to a monastery, whereas Jesus and John preached to the whole population and did not exhort their hearers to withdraw from society. . . . Nevertheless, many ideas and expressions in the Gospels have parallels in the Dead Sea Scrolls [written by the Essenes of Qumran,] that illuminate the teaching of Jesus and highlight more clearly the Jewish roots of his teaching.

Still another possibility is that Jesus never lived at Qumran but simply read and was influenced by Essene doctrines.

In whatever context and manner Jesus's philosophy and values developed, he was baptized by the traveling preacher John the Baptist in the Jordan River. According to the Gospels, John was a relative of Jesus's who declared, "I am the voice of one crying in the wilderness, 'Make straight the way of the Lord.'" Christians interpret these words to mean that John was sent to prepare for the coming of the Messiah.

After his baptism, the Gospels say, Jesus gathered around himself the Twelve Apostles and traveled through the countryside. His sermons, containing instruction on how to live in service to God, often drew large crowds. It was through this mobile ministry that he became well known as a teacher and healer.

AT THE RIVER JORDAN

This version of Jesus's baptism comes from the Gospel of Matthew.

In those days came John the Baptist, preaching in the wilderness of Judea, 'Repent, for the kingdom of heaven is at hand.'. . . Now John wore a garment of camel's hair, and a leather girdle around his waist; and his food was locusts and wild honey. Then went out to him [Jews from] Jerusalem and all Judea . . . confessing their sins [and] then Jesus came from Galilee to the Jordan [River] to John, to be baptized by him.

Opposite Page: *The Baptism of Christ*, an 1873 print of Jesus being baptized by John the Baptist in the Jordan River

31

Eventually, the authorities in Jerusalem arrested Jesus. They may have viewed his ability to gather and impress large numbers of followers and admirers as a threat to their power and the established order. Whatever their motives were, sometime between 30 and 33 CE, they handed him over to Judea's Roman governor, Pontius Pilate. After a short hearing, Pilate ordered his crucifixion, a common method of capital punishment in those days. He was executed outside the city walls.

His Teachings

The Gospels reveal that during his brief public ministry Jesus delivered sermons about humane, morally upright concepts. He urged people to love one another and to seek and promote peace and brotherhood. He also called for treating the poor and downtrodden with respect, dignity, and charity.

The Sermon on the Mount is widely considered the most influential of his public addresses. When and where it took place is unclear, but its message of love, forgiveness, mercy, and fair treatment for those who are poor, weak, or persecuted has endured. It was in this sermon that Jesus expressed a variation of the so-called Golden Rule: "Judge not, that you be not judged," a saying that encapsulates the essence of Christian belief and doctrine.

Particularly controversial at the time, and no less today, was Jesus's conviction that force and violence were not the best ways to respond to evil and violence. He preached about this concept in the Sermon on the Mount, saying:

> You have heard that it was said [in Leviticus 24:20, in the Old Testament,] "An eye for an eye and a tooth for a tooth." But I say to you, Do not resist one who is

evil. But if any one strikes you on the right cheek, turn to him the other [cheek] also. And if anyone would sue you and take your coat, let him have your cloak as well.

These and Jesus's other teachings did not die with him. His Apostles and other followers kept them alive and passed them along to others. Originally their intention was not to start a new religion, but as Jesus's legacy grew and his following spread from Jews to Gentiles, the movement broke away from Judaism and set a new course.

Jesus teaching his disciples, as depicted in *The Sermon on the Mount* by Carl Heinrich Bloch

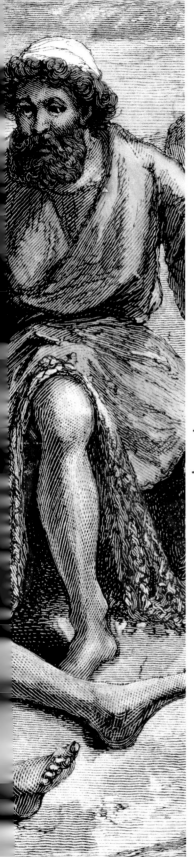

Chapter

3

The Mission to the Gentiles

Jesus's life and ministry are at the heart of Christianity. Equally important to the faith's organization and expansion, however, were his Apostles and Paul, one of Jesus's shrewdest and most energetic followers.

Peter and Andrew mending their nets by the Sea of Galilee before becoming disciples of Jesus, as portrayed in a hand-colored woodcut of a nineteenth-century illustration

Chief among the apostles was a fisherman named Simon, who took a leading position in the early church. Jesus changed his name from Simon to a name meaning "rock"—*Cephas* in Aramaic, *Peter* in Greek. Guided by a vision, Peter was the first to preach to and convert Gentiles, according to the Book of Acts. But he is best known as the apostle for the Jews. Paul, on the other hand, became a missionary to the Gentiles.

In the wake of Jesus's death, Paul's message reverberated beyond the fringes of the greater Mediterranean region, and over time thousands of Jews and non-Jews converted to Christianity as a result of his ministry. The vast majority of modern biblical scholars even consider Paul the principal founder of Christianity.

Paul's work was based on Jesus's teachings and the belief that Jesus was the Son of God. With a view to ensuring that these concepts would survive and spread, Paul took them to the Gentiles, an approach that Jesus himself had not tried. Some biblical scholars, such as A. N. Wilson, even suggest that Jesus had no intention of forming a new religion or globalizing his message. In his biography of Paul, Wilson expounds upon this point:

> When we have looked at the evidence, it will seem at the very least highly unlikely that Jesus . . . had any ambitions to found a world religion. All the indications are that this charismatic healer and preacher limited his sphere of activities to rural and exclusively Jewish regions. [In the Gospels] Jesus is quoted as saying that his mission is to 'the lost sheep of the house of Israel.'

Initially, Paul also appears not to have set out to create a new faith. Explains Justo González,

While he felt called to preach to the Gentiles, his usual procedure upon arriving at a new town was to go to the synagogue and the Jewish community. Again, he did not believe that he was preaching a new religion, but rather the fulfillment of the promises made to Israel. His message was not that Israel had been abandoned by God, but rather that now, through the resurrection of Jesus, the age of the Messiah had dawned, and that therefore the way was open for Gentiles to join the people of God.

The Resurrection and the Way

Although Jesus's teachings remained compelling and inspiring to some Jews after his execution, in the end it was reports of his resurrection from the dead that drew more people to the new movement. According to the Gospel of Luke, some of Jesus's friends went to his tomb three days after he was crucified and were amazed. "They found the stone [that had blocked the entrance] rolled away from the tomb, but when they went in they did not find the body." Later that same day, Luke says, Jesus appeared before his Apostles. "They were startled and frightened and supposed that they saw a spirit. And he said to them, 'Why are you troubled?'" After assuring them that he was really their friend Jesus, who had recently been crucified, he told them:

It is written, that the Christ should suffer and on the third day rise from the dead, and that repentance and forgiveness of sins should be preached in his name to all nations, beginning from Jerusalem. You are witnesses of these things. And behold, I send the promise of my Father [God] upon you.

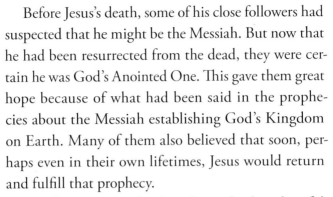

Before Jesus's death, some of his close followers had suspected that he might be the Messiah. But now that he had been resurrected from the dead, they were certain he was God's Anointed One. This gave them great hope because of what had been said in the prophecies about the Messiah establishing God's Kingdom on Earth. Many of them also believed that soon, perhaps even in their own lifetimes, Jesus would return and fulfill that prophecy.

For these reasons the Apostles and other close followers of Jesus may have seen themselves as Judaism's vanguard—a special, chosen group of Jews to serve as leaders. Numbering no more than a few hundred, they called themselves the people of "the Way." (The term *Christian* was not coined until several years later.) The exact meaning of this name is unclear. But it likely referred to the "way," or path, to God's approaching Kingdom; Jesus's followers may have seen themselves as the guardians of that path."

Jesus's claim created a problem, however. Most other Jews did not accept that Jesus was the "Way." Tensions increased and then came to a head when a devout member of the Way named Stephen enraged the Jewish leaders in Jerusalem. Stephen accused them of conspiring to murder Jesus and warned that they and the great Jewish Temple would be destroyed in the coming apocalypse. The leaders reacted vengefully. So they ordered Stephen's execution.

A painting of Jesus resurrected from the grave, to the astonishment of the soldiers guarding his tomb

Paul's Conversion

After Stephen's death, many of the other members of the Way were persecuted. The Apostles Peter and John were beaten and ordered to stop preaching, and a number of others fled to Damascus and Antioch, in Syria. (A few members of the Way stayed in Jerusalem, where Jesus's brother James led them.) Even in Syria, the persecutions continued. One of the most enthusiastic

tormentors was a Jew named Saul of Tarsus, who eventually took the name Paul. He later admitted: "I persecuted [the] Way to the death, binding and delivering to prison both men and women, [and] I journeyed to Damascus to take those also who were there and bring them in bonds to Jerusalem to be punished."

It was during that journey to Damascus, likely in the year 36, that Paul's life changed forever. He later recalled,

La Conversion de Saint Paul, a 1690 painting by Luca Giordano

About noon, a great light from heaven suddenly shone about me. And I fell to the ground and heard a voice saying to me, 'Saul, Saul, why do you persecute me?' And I answered, 'Who are you, Lord?' And he said to me, 'I am Jesus of Nazareth whom you are persecuting.' Now those who were with me saw the light but did not hear the voice. . . . And I said, 'What shall I do, Lord?' And the Lord said to me, 'Rise and go into Damascus, and there you will be told all that is appointed for you to do.'

JESUS DEFINES THE MISSION

In one of several recollections of his vision on the road to Damascus, Paul, as quoted in the Book of Acts, stated that the idea to preach to the Gentiles came directly from Jesus, who said:

I have appeared to you for this purpose, to appoint you to serve and bear witness to the things in which you have seen me and to those in which I will appear to you delivering you from the people and from the Gentiles—to whom I send you to open their eyes, that they may turn from darkness to light [and] that they may receive forgiveness of sins and a place among those who are sanctified by faith in me.

At the time, the idea of sharing the news of Jesus's divinity and teachings with the Gentiles was not new. Members of the Way in Jerusalem and Antioch had already envisioned doing so, but no concerted effort had yet been made. Paul's mission would break important new ground.

Reaching Out to Gentiles

The main reason that the Way had not reached out to Gentiles was that its members expected Gentiles to convert to Judaism when joining their group—an expectation that proved to be unreasonable. Jews had certain customs that most Gentiles viewed as too rigorous, or distasteful, or even somewhat terrifying. They followed strict dietary laws, for instance, and practiced circumcision. On account of the drastic changes that conversion would entail, most of the Gentiles whom Paul and his associates initially approached refused to join the Way.

It did not take Paul long to see that the Way would fail to attract many converts if it kept its strict requirements for joining, especially circumcision. He persuaded the elders of the Way's chapter in Jerusalem to modify their strategy in about 49 CE. In the years that followed, Paul and other leading preachers and teachers journeyed across the Roman Empire, taking advantage of its excellent road network. They gained many new converts in Palestine, Asia Minor, Greece, Italy, and possibly even far-away Spain.

During all of his traveling and preaching, Paul never aimed to create or drum up support for a new religion. He remained confident that the era of the Messiah and God's Kingdom were close at hand. His intent seems to have been to show both Jews and non-Jews the best path to God. Within a generation or two, Paul apparently believed, all who revered Jesus and God would be enjoying the fruits of a hugely transformed world.

That large-scale, divine transformation did not occur, however. Instead there resulted a major split between Jewish and Gentile members of the Way. By the mid-50s CE, the non-Jewish members had come to call themselves Christians, and as they continued to grow in number, the Jewish Christians became less numerous. Their leader James was killed in Jerusalem in 62. And many members of his flock packed up and moved to Pella, a town far to the north on the right bank of the Jordan River. Then, four years later, most Jews in Palestine rebelled against Rome and in the bloody turmoil that followed a majority of the Jewish Christians

LAST OF THE JEWISH CHRISTIANS

J. R. Porter sums up the unfortunate fate of the Jewish Christians in the latter half of the first century:

> *The destruction of Jerusalem by the Romans in 70 CE was the principal cause of the decline in Jewish Christianity, and determined that in the future the church would be a predominantly Gentile body. [After the Roman attack on Jerusalem] Jewish Christianity was increasingly marginalized and fragmented. Various sects survived until at least 300 CE in different parts of the [Middle] East. . . . The best-known Jewish Christian group, the Ebionites, lived in [Jordan] and their name probably means "the poor." [They] were "adoptionists," believing that Jesus became Messiah and Son of God only when the Spirit [of God] entered him at his baptism.*

were killed. Only a few pockets of them survived in the deserts of Jordan and elsewhere, and within three centuries virtually all of them had died out.

Gentile Christians in various sectors of the Mediterranean world heard about the slaughter of Jews in Palestine. Hoping not

to be mistaken for Jews and fall victim to Rome's wrath, many of these Gentile followers of Jesus distanced themselves from Judaism. This hastened the already ongoing separation between Gentile and Jewish Christians, and by the late first century the Gentile branch of Christianity had become completely dominant.

Paul's mission to the Gentiles facilitated the spread of the Way beyond Palestine and accelerated the formation of Christianity as a new religion. "It guaranteed the survival of this faith," Wilson writes, "in worlds which were quite alien, spiritually and geographically, to its native setting of first-century Palestinian Judaism." In the time of Paul's ministry Christianity had grown from a small Jewish group to a potentially large-scale faith.

An apostle preaching about Christianity, as portrayed in an illustration based on a painting by Italian Renaissance painter Fra Angelico.

Chapter

4

Early Organization and Worship

By 100 CE, sixty to seventy years after Jesus's death, the new Christian faith had largely separated from Judaism. In a sense, the split was (and even today remains) incomplete because Christians retained a number of Jewish beliefs and writings. Nevertheless, most Christians increasingly were Gentiles who did not identify themselves as Jews.

Another significant change involved relocation. Christians were no longer concentrated in Judea. The faith had spread, first into Syria and other parts of the Middle East, and then westward into other Roman provinces. Initially these far-flung Christian communities survived on account of their members' strong

St. Paul Writing His Epistles, a sixteenth-century painting on display in a museum in Houston, Texas.

faith, courage, and determination. "In 100 AD ," theologian Tony Lane points out, the church was a relatively unorganized "small minority":

> While the Gospels and epistles were in circulation, they had not yet been gathered together to form a 'New Testament.' While there were brief affirmations of faith like 'Jesus is Lord,' there was no formal creed to be recited. The organization of the church was still fluid and varied from region to region, [and] finally, there were no set forms of worship.

In the years that followed, however, the Christian movement began organizing and its system of beliefs and worship solidified with surprising speed. Driving this development were those church leaders who came to be called the Apostolic

Fathers. Continuing the course plotted by Paul and the other Apostles, they established elements of worship and chose many of the sacred writings that remain cornerstones of Christian liturgy today.

Standard Beliefs and Unity

One of the first of these elements of worship to emerge was a statement that outlined the faith's core beliefs. Then called the Symbol of the Faith, and later the Apostles' Creed, it was composed in Rome around 150. Its purpose was to formalize the church's principles and to distinguish "true" believers from people who claimed to be Christian but held false beliefs. The main tenets of the creed were often organized into a set of three questions that church leaders posed to new members on the occasion of their baptism:

Do you believe in God the Father almighty?

Do you believe in Christ Jesus, the Son of God, our Lord, who was born of the Holy Ghost and of Mary the virgin, who was crucified under Pontius Pilate, and died, and rose again at the third day, living from among the dead, and ascended unto heaven and sat on the right of the Father and will come to judge the quick and the dead?

Do you believe in the Holy Ghost, the holy church, and the resurrection of the flesh?

The ceremony of baptism, along with the formal questions containing the creed, were part of a larger attempt to standardize the church's system of worship. Having a common standard was vital during these formative years because Christian communities were distant from one another and news traveled slowly. Communities that were out of touch with the main centers in Rome and Antioch tended to develop their own variations of core beliefs and rituals, an outcome that a number of church leaders felt would divide and weaken the movement over time.

Particularly influential among these early leaders was the head of the Christian enclave in Antioch, Ignatius (who died in 107). He was the first person to call the church "catholic," or "having universally accepted principles and customs." Ignatius wrote letters to various Christian communities and urged harmony among them. "You should live in an unblameable unity," he said. "Being joined together in concord and harmonious love, of which Jesus Christ is the Captain and Guardian, do ye, man by man, become but one choir."

Church Leadership

Ignatius and other Apostolic Fathers also helped establish a hierarchy of leadership and authority within the church. This system marked the beginnings of the clergy. Community elders oversaw a majority of early Christian communities. They held the title of presbyter, from the Greek word *presbuteros,* meaning "old man." Along with their assistants, called deacons, the presbyters, or priests, ran the weekly and yearly affairs of the local churches.

Frequently, several individual churches sprang up within a larger Christian community or district (later called a diocese), and it became necessary for an authoritative official to administer each district. These higher-ranking clergymen came to be called bishops (from the Greek word *episkopos,* meaning "over-seer"). One important duty of the early bishops, who were elected by the priests and members of the community, was to oversee the rituals and special services of worship. A bishop also managed the lands and cemeteries owned by the churches in his district. In addition, he stayed in contact with his fellow bishops so as to maintain the unity of Christian policies and beliefs. Eventually, bishops began holding periodic meetings, called councils, in which they discussed and sometimes changed church policies.

At first, all bishops were equal in rank, but over time the bishop of Rome came to embody special prestige and author-ity. His title—Pope—was derived from the Greek word *pappas,* meaning "father."

The early bishops and other clergymen lived off funds offered by the worshipers in their districts. British journalist and histo-rian Brian Moynahan explains the financial situation that devel-oped among the Christian communities:

> The flow of funds [from the worshipers] was encour-aged by reminders that contributions were aids to the remission of sins. Fixed clerical salaries were at first con-sidered an 'outrage,' but they became a regular practice. A system of tithes evolved, based on the one used by the Jews to support their landless Levite priests, in which a tenth of livestock, food produce, or income from trade was given each year. . . . At Rome, funds were split in four between the bishop, the remaining clergy, the main-tenance of buildings, and widows, paupers, and virgins.

WHAT CLERGYMEN WORE

Scholar Henry Chadwick here describes the evolution of
the outfits worn by clergymen.

*The clergy did not initially wear special vestments; they were
simply instructed to see that what they wore was 'wholly clean'.
By the third century it became common for at least some clergy
. . . to wear either white or black. One group in fourth-century*

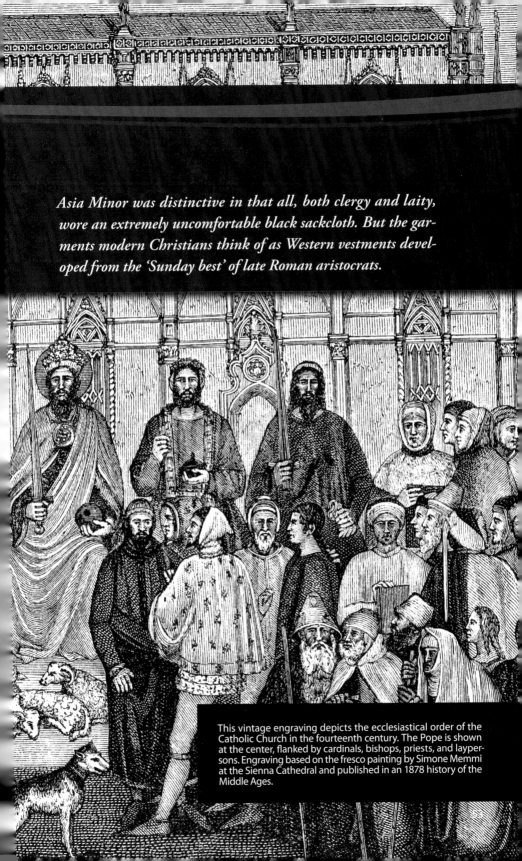

Asia Minor was distinctive in that all, both clergy and laity, wore an extremely uncomfortable black sackcloth. But the garments modern Christians think of as Western vestments developed from the 'Sunday best' of late Roman aristocrats.

This vintage engraving depicts the ecclesiastical order of the Catholic Church in the fourteenth century. The Pope is shown at the center, flanked by cardinals, bishops, priests, and laypersons. Engraving based on the fresco painting by Simone Memmi at the Sienna Cathedral and published in an 1878 history of the Middle Ages.

Early Christian Services

Worship services led by the clergy took place on Sunday, a tradition adopted because it was said that Jesus had risen from the dead on a Sunday. Services were also held on Wednesday and Friday. These were seen as days of sorrow because they marked Judas's betrayal of Jesus.

Formal church buildings did not exist yet, so initially the ceremonies were held in private homes. Such houses most often consisted of a large main room with a big table at one end. The bishop or head priest sat behind the table in a central position and the lower-ranking clergy were seated to his left and right. In front of and facing them sat the members of the local community, called the congregation. At first men and women had separate seating sections, as did widows, virgins, and slaves.

The exact nature and order of the rituals in these early services remain unclear, but based on extensive research and some educated guessing, modern scholars think an average service started with prayers and hymn-singing. Then came a reading from the Jewish Scriptures, the Gospels, or other sacred writings. Printed copies of these accounts and writings did not yet exist, so readings were the only way most worshipers could learn the contents of these texts.

Following the reading likely came the central ritual of the service—the Eucharist, the act of communion. It consisted of worshipers eating a small piece of bread, which symbolized Jesus's body, and drinking a little wine, which symbolized his blood. Accompanying the Eucharist ceremony was a prayer in which the priest or bishop engaged the congregation. A surviving example reads in part:

Bishop: The Lord be with you.

People: And with your spirit.

Bishop: Lift up your hearts.

People: We lift them up to the Lord. . . .

Bishop: Let us give thanks to the Lord.

People: It is right and meet.

Bishop: We give thanks, O God, through your beloved son Jesus Christ . . . who when he was betrayed . . . took bread and gave thanks to you and said: "Take, eat, this is my body which is broken for you. Likewise also the cup, saying: this is my blood which is shed for you. When you do this, do it in remembrance of me."

EXCLUDING WOMEN FROM LEADERSHIP

It appears that in some early Christian communities women at first served in the clergy (though never as bishops); but as time went on male authorities increasingly frowned on this practice, as explained by religious studies professor at Stonehill College, Michael D. Coogan:

The [eventual] message to women in the churches was clear: find your proper place and stay there. Such a warning would have been unnecessary unless women were doing the opposite, involving themselves in leadership roles at the expense of the reputation of the churches. The undisputed letters of Paul provide ample evidence for women as active and vocal leaders in the churches [and] make it clear that women apostles were viewed as heroes in some churches. [But some leading bishops] attempted to . . . limit the rights and roles of women in the churches, and for most of Christian history they have been successful.

Creating a Canon

The Gospels and Eucharist prayers read aloud during worship services were not the only Christian writings emerging. Clergymen also read from Paul's letters (also called the Pauline Epistles). Many of these were named for local congregations to whom he had preached, including Romans, Galatians, and First and Second Corinthians. In addition, dozens of other letters, texts, stories, and collections of sayings about Jesus and his Apostles circulated through the Empire in the early second century.

Initially, no comprehensive collection, or canon (from the Greek word *kanon*), of these writings existed. But in the middle of the century, bishops in various parts of the realm began moving to compile single-volume collections. The texts contained in these compilations varied from community to community; but over the course of several decades, in what was a painstaking process, an overall consensus steadily emerged. By the year 200 a basic New Testament canon had crystallized. In addition to the Gospels of Matthew, Mark, Luke, and John, it contained the book of Acts, twelve of Paul's letters, Jude's letter, and two of John's letters.

With the completion of the New Testament and standardization of weekly services and rituals, the new faith had, from an organizational standpoint, carved an identity for itself. Despite this progress, Christians still had a major obstacle in their path. It was the fact that they were widely hated by many pagan Romans, who sometimes persecuted Christians. If the faith was to survive, it would have to be defended. And several brave members stepped forward and risked, and in some cases lost, their lives to do so. If the faith were to survive, it would have to overcome the pagan status quo in the Roman world.

An antique, hand-colored print of early Christians reading a scroll in the time of the Roman Empire.

Chapter

5

Persecutors and Apologists

In the late first century, Christian communities across the Roman Empire worked not only to organize and spread their faith, but also to forge their religious and cultural identities in Roman society. From then until the early fourth century, the new movement encountered waves of persecution. These brief but brutal episodes of abuse were usually random, with long interludes of calm and relative safety between them, and it was not unusual for the authorities to target Christians in one region while leaving those in other parts of the Empire alone. By and large, Christians found themselves fighting for survival.

The Roman government singled out Christians for reasons that are widely misunderstood today. The chief misconception is that Roman officials were intolerant of faiths outside of Rome's state religion. In actuality, the Romans were one of the most religiously tolerant peoples in history. Over time they folded into their religious system a diverse range of gods and beliefs, including some that originated in Egypt, Asia Minor, Iran, and other foreign regions. The average Roman worshiped one or more deities of his or her choosing on a regular basis. For example, one might be a devout follower of the Egyptian goddess Isis, but he or she would also acknowledge that other people's gods, including Rome's state gods, were no less real and worthy. The general view was that there were numerous acceptable paths to a few universal religious truths.

Against this backdrop of religious freedom, the Romans' mistrust of Christians had nothing to do with faith-based intolerance; instead, it was socially based. "To understand the persecution of the Christians," notes the late University of Michigan historian Chester G. Starr, "one must turn to the practical reasons why they were disliked on the popular level and also by the imperial government."

Motives for Persecution

Some of the worst injustices committed against the early Christians were founded upon misunderstandings about their rituals and ceremonies. In general these services were held in private and were open only to Christians or those interested in joining the faith. Worshiping in private was not unusual, and rumors steadily spread that some of these meetings featured anti-social, illegal, and even barbaric practices. According to the late Yale Divinity School professor Kenneth S. Latourette,

> [the Christians] were popularly charged with perpe-
> trating the grossest immoralities in their conventicles.
> It was said that both sexes met together at night [and]
> that promiscuous intercourse followed. Garbled reports
> circulated of the central Christian rite, the Eucharist.
> . . . [Rumors held] that Christians regularly sacrificed
> an infant and consumed its blood and flesh. [That]
> Christians called one another brother and sister and
> loved one another on the scantiest acquaintance was
> regarded as evidence of vice.

These rumors were not true—yet many people, especially those who had never met a Christian, believed them.

Another reason Christians were disliked was that they tended to avoid popular public festivals and events. They objected to the honoring of pagan gods that occurred at such events. "Because they refused to participate in pagan ceremonies," continues Latourette, "Christians were dubbed atheists. Through their abstention from much of the community life . . . they were derided. . . ." Most non-Christians assumed Christians were anti-social, and over time Christians developed a reputation for having *odium generis humani,* a "hatred for the human race."

Early Christians appeared to be anti-social for another reason. In the eyes of most pagans, their attitude toward their own god made them seem highly intolerant of others' beliefs. Christians believed that their god was the only one that existed and that the gods of other faiths were false. Non-Christians tended to view this attitude as disrespectful and even offensive. Some pagans worried that having a community of "atheists" in their midst might cause their own gods to punish the Empire.

In Roman government, high-level officials were also wary of Christians because they refused to worship the emperor. Few, if any, Romans believed their emperors were actually divine beings, but for political reasons the state maintained that fiction. People who refused to acknowledge it were sometimes seen as possible threats to public order.

CHRISTIANS MENTALLY INFERIOR?

Some non-Christian Romans even looked down on Christians because they thought they were intellectually inferior. Justo Gonzalez explains:

Christians were an ignorant lot whose doctrines, although preached under a cloak of wisdom, were foolish and even self-contradictory. This seems to have been a common attitude among the cultured aristocracy, for whom Christians were a despicable rabble. . . . Furthermore—the argument went on—the Jewish and Christian God is ridiculous. They claim on the one hand that God is omnipotent, high above every creature. But on the other hand they depict God as a busybody who is constantly delving into human affairs, who goes into every home listening to what is said and even checking what is being cooked. This is sheer contradiction and nonsense.

Varied Approaches to Persecution

Pagan Romans considered Christians at the least as anti-social, suspicious characters, and at the worst as criminals and troublemakers. Such views were more than enough to fuel the periodic persecutions that occurred for some two and a half centuries. Emperor Nero instigated the first organized campaign against Christians. He ruled from 54 CE to 68 CE, when Christians made up only a tiny proportion of the Empire's population. In 64 a terrible fire ravaged the capital city of Rome. When rumors spread that Nero had started the blaze, which was almost certainly untrue, he saw the Christians as an easy scapegoat and blamed them. As the first-century Roman historian Tacitus described it:

> [Nero] punished with every refinement the notoriously depraved Christians. . . . First, [he] had self-acknowledged Christians arrested. Then on their information, large numbers of others were condemned. . . . Their deaths were made farcical. Dressed in wild animals' skins, they were torn to pieces by dogs, or crucified, or made into torches to be ignited after dark as substitutes for daylight. . . . Despite their guilt as Christians . . . the victims were pitied. For it was felt that they were being sacrificed to one man's brutality rather than to the national interest.

Most later Christian persecutions were widely seen as justified, however. This is because the larger the Christian movement became, the more anti-Christian

Bust of Nero at the Capitoline Museum, Rome

rumors spread and the more that movement was perceived as a potential threat to society.

Cruel crackdowns on Christians took place under the emperors Domitian (81–96), Marcus Aurelius (161–180), Septimius Severus (193–211), Decius (250–251), and some later emperors.

Other emperors refrained from ordering large-scale persecutions, but did prosecute Christians on a random, individual basis. In such cases, the government more or less followed the example set by the emperor Trajan (98–117). Around 112, the Roman provincial governor Pliny the Younger requested Trajan's advice on how

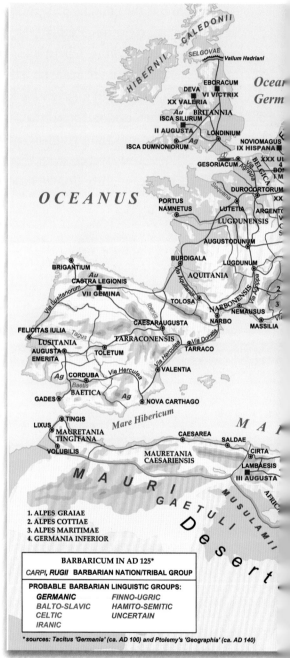

1. ALPES GRAIAE
2. ALPES COTTIAE
3. ALPES MARITIMAE
4. GERMANIA INFERIOR

BARBARICUM IN AD 125*
CARPI, RUGII BARBARIAN NATION/TRIBAL GROUP

PROBABLE BARBARIAN LINGUISTIC GROUPS:
GERMANIC   FINNO-UGRIC
BALTO-SLAVIC   HAMITO-SEMITIC
CELTIC   UNCERTAIN
IRANIC

*sources: Tacitus 'Germania' (ca. AD 100) and Ptolemy's 'Geographia' (ca. AD 140)

THE ROMAN EMPIRE IN AD 125

	IMPERIAL BORDER
■	LEGIONARY BASE
VII CLAUDIA	LEGION DEPLOYED (125 AD)
	MAJOR NAVAL BASE
GALATIA	ROMAN PROVINCE
◉	ROMAN CITY
Via Appia / Vetus	MAIN ROAD
Au	GOLD DEPOSITS
Ag	SILVER DEPOSITS
COLCHIS	ROMAN CLIENT STATE

6000 m
2000 m
1500 m
1000 m
400 m
200 m
0 m

0   250   500   750   1000
kilometers

The Christian Martyrs' Last Prayer, an 1883 oil on canvas by Jean-Léon Gérôme

to handle Christians. Trajan, who was far more humane than Nero, said:

These people must not be hunted out. If they are brought before you and the charge against them is proved, they must be punished, but in the case of anyone who denies that he is a Christian . . . he is to be pardoned as a result of this repentance however suspect his past conduct may be. But pamphlets [containing lists of accused Christians] circulated anonymously must play no part in any accusation. They create the worst sort of precedent and are quite out of keeping with the spirit of our age.

Though far from enlightened by modern standards, this policy established a legal procedure by which Christians who were arrested could avoid punishment: if they renounced Jesus Christ and promised to offer prayers to the emperor, they were spared. A few accused Christians chose this way out; most others, however, demonstrated courage and held fast to their convictions. Over time, thousands received death sentences and became martyrs to the faith. Some of the victims were burned alive, others crucified, and still others killed by gladiators or wild animals during public games.

THE MAKING OF A MARTYR

Among the Christians who died and became martyrs during the persecution enacted by Marcus Aurelius was a woman named Blandina. According to the account of a later Christian writer, Eusebius, who did not witness the event, Blandina underwent a number of humiliating and painful tortures before a crowd in a Roman amphitheater. After being whipped and exposed to the heat of a fire, Eusebius wrote, "she finally was placed in a net and thrown to a bull. She was tossed about for some time by the animal but was insensitive to what was happening to her because of her hope and . . . her communion with Christ. . . . And the [spectators] themselves confessed that never had a woman among them suffered so many and such horrible tortures."

Defenders of the Faith

Some Christians tried to stop the persecutions by writing apologies. In ancient times an apology was a document that explained and defended someone's beliefs or actions. The Christian apologists hoped to make non-Christians understand what Christianity stood for and to eliminate the common prejudices against the faith.

Among the more influential apologists were Justin (ca. 100–165), Tertullian (ca. 160–240), and Origen (184–254). Justin dismissed many of the negative rumors about Christians and argued that they were loyal, not threatening, to Rome. Tertullian joined Justin in maintaining that Christians were patriotic and added that he and his fellow Christians had been terribly misunderstood. "We are held to be criminals [and] deceivers," he wrote,

"and are accused of having sworn to murder babies and to eat them and of committing adulterous acts. . . . This is the witness you bring forth against us. [Over time the rumors have] hardened into a matter of opinion, [but] it has not yet been [proven, so] I call on the steadfastness of nature itself against those who assume that such accusations against us are credible."

A few pagan Romans learned to live in peace with Christians, but a great many others remained convinced that Christians were a menace. Persecutions continued and the faith grew slowly, though steadily, in its first couple of centuries. That regrettable situation did not endure. They eventually encountered an emperor they respected. More importantly, he respected them.

The Persecution of the First Christians, by Giuseppe Mancinelli. The painting is on display at the Museum of Capodimonte in Naples, Italy.

Chapter

6

The Faith Finds a Friend

Christians survived two centuries of persecutions at the hands of the Roman government and its citizens. However, the fledgling religion survived because it strongly appealed to the poor and underprivileged.

Cambridge University scholar L. P. Wilkinson said that Christianity offered people of all social classes, even slaves, "a simple and joyful message of love and hope . . . love of a savior who had quite recently lived man's life [and] hope of an eternity of bliss for believers as a compensation for the trials of this life. Their community was a haven for the lonely, [and] finally, they prospered just because they were persecuted, [as] their suffering drew them together for comfort and in loyalty."

Fortunately for the struggling faith, however, near the start of the fourth century it suddenly gained favor from Rome's highest ruler: Emperor Constantine, who governed from 306 to 337. During his long reign, he granted Christians economic privileges and legal protection against discrimination. He eventually converted to Christianity and went on to commission the building of numerous churches and even an entire city in celebration of the faith. His deeds and his testimony legitimized Christianity in Roman society and positioned the faith to become a major religious, as well as social and political, force.

If Christianity had remained confined to the outer spheres of Roman society, it likely would have had little chance of spreading—much less of transforming the Empire's social and political status quo. "It is certainly likely," asserts historian Charles Freeman, "that without imperial support, Christianity would never have been more than the religion of a minority." For these reasons, Freeman continues, Constantine's support of Christians marked what in retrospect is seen as "an important turning point in the history of the Western world."

The Great Persecution

It remains unclear how and when Constantine initially befriended Christians, but it appears that the relationship began when he was fairly young. He and his father, the noted Roman general Constantius, lived in the city of Trier, in Rome's province of Gaul. (At the time the province encompassed most of modern-day France, though today Trier is situated in Germany.) At some point, it seems, the two men bonded with some local Gallic Christians, an alliance that was to have enormous consequences during the series of dramatic political events that followed.

In 293 the reigning emperor, Diocletian, divided imperial power among four men, including himself. This created a ruling coalition called the "Tetrarchy," in which Diocletian retained the senior position of authority. As one of the four tetrarchs, Constantius ruled Gaul and Britain, with Trier as his capital.

Constantius tolerated the Christians in his provinces, so they enjoyed a fair measure of peace and security. But Christians in other parts of the Empire were less fortunate.

Bust of Constantine

Diocletian, who ruled much of the Empire's eastern realm, was, like so many Roman leaders before him, suspicious of Christians. He was well aware of rumors circulating about Christians committing incest during their rituals and worried that such crimes and other misconducts might anger Jupiter and the traditional state gods, whom he revered.

A modern illustrator's depiction of the persecution of early Christians

For a while, Diocletian did not act on his suspicions, but at a customary state religious ceremony in 303, he discerned some troubling omens during an animal sacrifice. The Roman priests laid the blame on the Christians, claiming they had put a magical hex on the ceremony. Spurred by another tetrarch, Galerius, the angry Diocletian launched the biggest, bloodiest anti-Christian persecution ever. All Christian churches were closed; Christian documents were burned; and many members of the faith were imprisoned or executed.

WITNESS TO THE PERSECUTION

Fourth-century Christian bishop and writer Eusebius described what he recalled from the persecution ordered by Diocletian and Galerius:

We saw with our own eyes the houses of prayer thrown down to the very foundations, and the Divine and Sacred Scriptures committed to the flames in the midst of the market-places. . . . And royal edicts were published everywhere, commanding that the churches be leveled to the ground [and] that all the rulers of the churches in every place be first thrown into prison. . . . Of the rest each one endured different forms of torture. The body of one was scourged with rods. Another was punished [by being put on the rack and] suffered a miserable death [while others] were struck in the mouth and silenced.

Meanwhile, Christians in the West largely escaped persecution. Constantius closed the churches in his provinces, but did not arrest or harass anyone. Constantine continued his father's policy of moderate tolerance when he replaced him as ruler of Gaul in 306.

A New God on His Side

In 305 Diocletian voluntarily abdicated the throne. He hoped that a new tetrarchy would form and enact a smooth transition of power; to his regret, power was not transferred smoothly and a large-scale civil war soon erupted at the hands of several Roman strongmen. Some of them, including Constantine, declared themselves emperor or were proclaimed emperor by their troops.

In 312, at the height of the conflict, one of the self-proclaimed sovereign rulers, Maxentius, captured Rome. Aiming to drive him out, Constantine led a large army toward the city. Constantine's men bore shields with a special insignia, the Christian symbol of Chi and Rho, which stood for the first two letters of the Greek name for Christ, *Christos*. Eusebius later claimed that the day before, Constantine and some of his troops had seen a huge cross of light in the sky, near the sun. "In his sleep [that night] the Christ of God appeared to [Constantine] with the same sign which he had seen in the heavens, and commanded him to make a likeness of that sign which he had seen in the heavens, and to use it as a safeguard in all engagements with his enemies."

It remains unknown whether Constantine's celestial vision and dream were real or whether Eusebius fabricated them later. Most modern historians agree that if the cross in the sky *was* real, it may have been a solar halo. Caused by the fall of ice crystals across the sun's rays, this optical phenomenon occasionally takes the form of a large cross of light.

What is more certain is that Constantine defeated his rival. The two armies clashed at Rome's Milvian Bridge. Thousands of Maxentius's soldiers drowned in the Tiber River and Constantine took the city. His good fortune in this battle convinced Constantine that the Christian God was not only real but also favored him. He was not convinced, however, that this deity was the sole god, nor did he at this point consider becoming a Christian. It was quite common for Roman rulers to honor and worship several gods at once, so as to appeal to all the Empire's peoples. Constantine kept with this practice. For example, he struck coins dedicated to traditional Roman gods, including Jupiter and the Unconquered Sun, for almost another decade.

Constantine was not quick to forget his seemingly fateful encounter with Christ and subsequent victory in Rome. He believed the Christian god had aided him and he felt it was only right to continue befriending that deity's followers. The renowned Cambridge University historian A. H. M. Jones summed up Constantine's outlook and the far-reaching consequences of his eventual conversion:

> Constantine knew and cared nothing for the metaphysical and ethical teaching of Christianity when he became a devotee of the Christian God: he simply wished to enlist on his side a powerful divinity, Who had, he believed, spontaneously offered him a sign. His conversion was initially due to a meteorological phenomenon which he happened to witness at a critical moment of his career. But this fortuitous event ultimately led to Constantine's genuinely adopting the Christian Faith, to the conversion of the Roman Empire, and to the Christian civilization of Europe.

Increasing Support for the Christians

Constantine's first reward to his Christian friends came in the form of a decree granting them toleration. He issued the new law jointly with Valerius Licinius, who was on the verge of winning in the civil war's eastern theater after Constantine had emerged victorious in the West. The two rulers met in February 313 at Milan, in northern Italy. Although the decree was officially issued later in a different city, it retained the title of Edict of Milan.

Only three years later, the alliance between the two emperors crumbled and another civil war ensued. Constantine triumphed over Valerius Licinius and became sole ruler of the Empire in 324. By this time, though still not officially a Christian, he had come to accept many Christian principles and to support the faith and its members at every turn. He frequently met with the bishops and helped to settle some of their disputes. He also established Constantinople, "the city of Constantine," on the Bosphorus Strait, along the southern rim of the Black Sea. Dedicated to Jesus's mother, Mary, and the Holy Trinity (God the father, Son, and Holy Spirit) in May 330, the new metropolis became the Empire's eastern capital and Constantine subsequently devoted huge sums of money to building churches across the realm.

Constantine's greatest favor to the Christians was his conversion to their religion on his deathbed early in 337. This profession of faith set a precedent that proved momentous, for all but one of the emperors who followed him were Christians, too. In this way, the friendship of a powerful man enabled Christianity to overcome its poor reputation and status as a persecuted fringe movement, to grow and prosper, and eventually to become the dominant religion in the western world. For Christians, claimed Brian Moynahan, "the conversion of Constantine [was] as miraculous as that of Paul. It, too, shifted the course of world history."

FROM BASILICAS TO CHURCHES

Historian Charles Freeman penned this overview of Constantine's church-building program.

All over the empire new churches appeared. . . . Many were built over the shrines of martyrs, places which had been venerated since the early days of the church. Others took over prime sites within the major cities—even the sites of earlier imperial palaces—while Constantinople was planned as a Christian city. Churches now became magnificent treasure houses, objects of awe and inspiration of worship. . . . [For their design] there was a pagan model to copy: the basilica, typically a long hall with a flat timber roof and aisles running along its length. For centuries the basilicas had been used as law courts [but] now they were to receive a new function. . . . The greatest of the basilicas was St. Peter's in Rome, constructed over the shrine which for generations was believed to be the resting place of St. Peter's body.

Interior of St. Peter's, Rome, a 1731 oil painting by Giovanni Paolo Pannini. On display at the St. Louis Art Museum in St. Louis, Missouri.

Chapter

7

Rethinking Religious Beliefs

During the fourth century and on into the early fifth century, Christianity underwent two far-reaching revolutions. One was its rapid rise to social prominence and political power in the Roman Empire; the other was a major rethinking of the faith's principles, rules, and customs of everyday life.

This large-scale process sowed controversy, and a number of new ideas, writings, splinter groups, and movements sprang up to challenge the church's accepted traditions. Several of these counter-revolutionary concepts came to be considered heresies. A heresy is an idea or a movement that contradicts, harms, or distorts accepted church doctrine. The most famous heresy of the age was the Arian movement, which redefined core Christian beliefs regarding Jesus's sovereignty and the nature of the Trinity. There did emerge, however, other, less controversial ideas that were not propagated to subvert the status quo, but rather to diversify the faith and enrich Christian culture.

At the forefront of this torrent of debate were a handful of brilliant bishops, writers, and other intellectuals, many of whom were newcomers to the faith. As Charles Freeman says, "the late fourth and early fifth centuries produced a number of profound thinkers who had been brought up in the traditional world of classical [Greco-Roman] learning, converted to Christianity, and then deployed their penetrating intellects in the service of the church." Some of their ideas were rejected while others won widespread acceptance. For good or ill, their work influenced basic doctrines that would define the church for centuries to come.

Giving Up Earthly Pleasures

One sub-movement that was at first met with great skepticism but eventually became accepted among the faithful was monasticism. It was based on the notion that one of the best ways to honor God was to devote oneself exclusively to his worship. Monasticism entailed withdrawing from society and living an ascetic existence—that is, one of extreme self-discipline and self-denial. Christians who took up this way of life were (and are) known as monks.

The idea of living a monk's life to grow closer to or please God was not new. The Essenes of the Qumran community in

Palestine were among a number of people who had chosen this path in the past. But in the fourth century, after Constantine instituted the policy of religious toleration, many thousands of Christians joined the Monastic movement and retreated to deserts, caves, and other remote areas. There, they led simple lives of solitude and hard work, into which they incorporated long hours of prayer and meditation.

Many of those who joined the Monastic movement were critical of Christianity's newfound popularity, a change which they believed produced a culture of hypocrisy within the church. As Christianity swept through the halls of power, some leaders of the time, among them Eusebius, gave voice to this feeling, asserting that Christianity had become a fashionable means for attaining riches, power, and high social status. Such people, echoes Justo González, had joined the faith in order to acquire "privilege and position, without caring to delve too deeply into the meaning of Christian baptism and life, [while] Bishops competed with each other after prestigious positions. The rich and powerful seemed to dominate the life of the church." In response, many of the more devout—and often, poorer—Christians left the organized church behind and became monks.

Initially, many church leaders frowned on the monastic movement. They wanted to retain control over their members, and they had little or no control over people living by themselves outside the confines of everyday society. Over time, however, bishops and other Christians came to accept and respect the monastic lifestyle. For example, Athanasius, a prominent bishop in the mid-fourth century, penned a biography of Anthony, a well-known Christian monk who dwelled in Egypt. Athanasius praised Anthony and others whose love for God inspired them to give up earthly pleasures. The monastic life remained a major aspect of the faith in medieval times and beyond.

St. Anthony—a detail from the *Visitation*, a painting by Italian Renaissance artist Piero di Cosimo. The complete painting shows Mary and St. Elizabeth, St. Nicholas, and St. Anthony.

A Simple, Difficult Life

For the monks who retreated to secluded regions of the Roman Empire in the fourth and fifth centuries, life was quiet, simple, and difficult. By choice, these ascetics lived in poverty, as they had given away most of their former possessions. Typically they made clothes and grew vegetables and other crops. They sold most of these commodities and used the money to buy essential items for the monastery or to help poor people in nearby villages. The daily routine for such a monk consisted almost entirely of manual labor in a field, workshop, or kitchen. During the few hours that were not spent working or sleeping, monks prayed, listened to religious sermons, sang hymns, or studied the Bible.

Controversies, Heresies, and Clarifications

There is no doubt that Christian leaders were far less worried about the monastic movement than they were about heresies and other serious threats to the faith, such as internal church politics. The first major controversy along these lines came about in 313, the same year that Constantine decreed religious toleration. The dispute began when Donatus, a bishop in Numidia (in North Africa), approached the emperor and asked him to block a priest named Caecilian from becoming a bishop. The Donatists, as the movement came to be known, claimed that Christian leaders who had allowed the Romans to seize the faith's holy books during Diocletian's persecution were traitors. The priest scheduled to make Caecilian a bishop was one of these alleged "betrayers of the faith." The ceremony, Donatus contended, would not be valid.

Most other bishops disagreed with Donatus, seeing him as a troublemaker. They persuaded Constantine to side with them and in 316 the emperor expelled the Donatists from their churches. This move was only partially effective, however, as the group continued to exist, mainly in North Africa, for three more centuries.

The Arian heresy proved to be an even graver threat to Christian doctrine. The movement's namesake was Arius, a priest who lived in Alexandria, Egypt. According to Michael Grant, Arius contended that "Jesus had not got quite the same qualifications as his divine Father. . . . Although [Jesus had been] created before time and superior to other creatures, [he] was like them changeable [and] consequently different in Essence from the Father . . . so that [Jesus] cannot, therefore, himself be God, to whom he is in a sense posterior [inferior or subservient]."

It was this observation that, as Grant says, "caused the storm, the most passionate storm that ever convulsed the Christian world, since it seemed to reduce the Son to a status that was less than divine."

In response to Arian, Constantine organized a large meeting of bishops in 325 at Nicea, in Asia Minor. (This so-called Council of Nicea was the first of seven "Ecumenical Councils" held by the early Roman Catholic Church.) After the more than two hundred bishops in attendance had presented their arguments, the emperor sided with the majority against the Arians. He urged the leadership to adopt the principle of *homoousios,* a

Greek word meaning "of the same substance." In the theological sense, it referred to the idea that Jesus and God were one and the same being. The Council issued a formal statement, known as the Nicene Creed, which signified their acceptance of the doctrine and rejection of Arianism.

THE NICENE CREED

The Nicene Creed issued by the Bishops at Nicea says in part:

We believe in one God, the Father almighty, maker of all things visible and invisible; And in one Lord, Jesus Christ, the Son of God, begotten of the Father, that is from the substance of the Father. He is God from God, light from light . . . begotten not made, of one substance [homoousios] with the Father. By him all things were made, things in heaven and on earth. . . . The holy catholic and apostolic Church anathematizes [denounces or curses] those who say: 'There was once when he was not,' and 'He was not, before he was begotten.'

In the wake of the dispute over Arianism, some bishops, writers, and church leaders used the ideas that had emerged out of the Nicene meetings to define theological concepts. Three bishops from Asia Minor—Basil of Caesarea, his younger brother Gregory of Nyssa, and their colleague Gregory of Nazianzus, together referred to as the Cappadocian Fathers—made the greatest contribution to the definition of God as a Trinity. Using biblical references and the idea of *homoousios,* they described God as triune: God the Father, Son and Holy Spirit (or Holy Ghost). Gregory of Nazianzus wrote:

> There are three individualities or hypostases, or, if you prefer, persons. . . . There is one substance—i.e., deity. For God is divided without division . . . and united in division. The Godhead is one in three and the three are one. . . . We must neither heretically fuse God together into one nor chop him up into inequality [as the Arians did].

Concerns About Moral Behavior

During the same period, other Christian thinkers helped to transform social and private attitudes to better reflect church-approved ethical and moral rules. Individuals including the noted philosopher Augustine (354-430) and the bishop Ambrose (ca. 337-397), an advisor to several emperors, were especially influential. They portrayed God as being deeply concerned with the behavior, attitudes, and even the thoughts of individual people.

As a result of these conservative Christian influences, Roman society slowly but steadily changed. Popular Roman pastimes such as chariot races, gladiatorial combats, the public baths, and gambling were increasingly frowned on. Also, divorce came to be seen as too easy to obtain. And sex, except by a married couple attempting to create children, was more and more viewed as sinful. Not all Christian social views were restrictive in nature, however. Charity for the poor and widows and orphans was strongly encouraged. And Christian leaders urged more humane treatment of slaves (although they accepted slavery itself as a fact of life).

Augustine's teachings also affected the way everyday people viewed their own behavior, responsibilities, and ultimate fate. He warned that God would send unrepentant sinners to Hell, where they would suffer eternal torment. He also crystallized the church's and society's views of original sin. All human beings, Augustine argued, are born as sinners because of Adam's sins against God in the Garden of Eden. So only by undergoing Christian baptism, which erased original sin, could a person make it into heaven.

A monk named Pelagius disagreed with Augustine. He contended that there was no such thing as original sin; people are by nature good. Although Pelagius made a name for himself, he was declared a heretic, and the emperor Honorius (who reigned from 395 to 423) made original sin an official church doctrine.

This and many other religious and social ideas preached by Christian thinkers in the fourth and fifth centuries became embedded in Western culture and thought.

A 1480 fresco by Sandro Botticelli showing St. Augustine in contemplation during prayer. On display at All-Saints Church in Florence, Italy.

Chapter

8

The Transformation of the State

By the fourth century, Christianity had transformed from a grassroots group into a pervasive movement with a large and influential following. As it spread throughout the Roman Empire, Christianity's reach and influence extended beyond the religious realm to permeate social and political life. As the fourth century progressed, Christians filled more and

The Colosseum in Rome

more high government positions and Christian rules, laws, and institutions replaced pagan ones.

In the span of only a few decades the once reviled and persecuted faith became the Empire's official religion. Its rise to prominence signaled the end of Rome's policy of tolerance toward all faiths, and Christianity became the only legal and legitimate religion. This comprehensive transformation was more than a remarkable reversal of fortunes; as Charles Freeman points out, it was also a significant historical turning point:

> The collaboration of the state with the only authorized religion [was] of fundamental importance. [The triumph of Christian] beliefs helped determine a framework of social, economic, spiritual, and cultural life which has persisted even into the [present] century. It is certainly arguable that, in this respect, the fourth century is one of the most influential in European history.

The Glamour of the Roman Name

The most critical key to Christianity's rapid rise to a position of authority in Rome's government was undoubtedly the acceptance of the faith by the emperors. Constantine's conversion in 337 set the initial precedent, and his three sons—Constantine II, Constantius II, and Constans—were raised as Christians so that the faith's foothold in the imperial palace remained strong.

The faith continued to win the favor of the richest, most powerful people in the realm. Constantine's three sons expanded the privileges their father had given Christian officials. In addition to tax exemptions for clergymen, Christian bishops were granted immunity from prosecution in the public courts; only their fellow bishops could try them. Constantine's sons also retained a ban their father had placed on pagan sacrifices.

AN UNBREAKABLE CHAIN TO TODAY

In his widely read book *Decline and Fall of the Roman Empire*, English historian Edward Gibbon asserts that Christianity's rise to power in Rome is one of the major revolutions of world history and that Constantine's pro-Christian policies from that time remain significant even today.

The victories and the civil policies of Constantine no longer influence the state of Europe; but a considerable portion of the globe still retains the impression which it received from the [religious] conversion of that monarch; and the ecclesiastical institutions of his reign are still connected, by an indissoluble [unbreakable] chain, with the opinions, the passions, and the interests of the present.

Bishops and other Christian leaders enjoyed not only new-found respect, but also the benefits of the ceremonial finery of Rome's imperial court. On the one hand, this luxury gave them a more exalted and authoritative image in the eyes of average Romans; on the other, it introduced new customs and rituals into Christian ceremony and worship. The clergy began burning incense, for instance. Burning spices and gums had long

The Baptism of Constantine, painted between 1517 and 1524 by the assistants of
the Italian Renaissance artist Raphael. Located in the Apostolic Palace, Vatican City.

been done at court out of respect for the emperor, but doing so
became an accepted gesture of reverence for God. Also, people
began bowing in submission to bishops, as royal courtiers had
traditionally bowed to the emperor. The bishops, who in the past
had dressed simply, adopted the elegant garb of Roman noble-
men from court.

The aura of power, mystery, and awe that Christianity gained
from the support of the emperors and the imperial court cannot
be overstated. Contends A. H. M. Jones,

the future of Christianity, its official adoption by the
empire was momentous, for Christianity thus acquired

the prestige and glamour of the Roman name; it became synonymous with that ancient civilization, whose grandiose buildings, stately ceremonial, luxurious life and ordered discipline fascinated [Rome's enemies, including] the uncouth barbarians of [northern Europe]. . . . They hankered to enter the charmed circle of the Roman world, their kings to become marshals of the empire and their warriors great landlords. . . . Inevitably they copied Roman ways, and with the rest of Roman culture adopted the Roman religion [Christianity].

Paganism Under Attack

Although Constantine's sons were pious Christians, the whole of Roman society did not always follow their lead. In the 340s and 350s a majority of Romans were still pagans, and many of them hoped that the recent imperial acceptance of Christianity was a passing trend that would soon fade. That hope seemed to be fulfilled when Constantius II died of illness in 361 and was succeeded by a distant relative, Julian. Julian was a committed pagan and sought to reverse the Christians' recent gains. He abolished the clergy's tax exemptions, re-instituted animal sacrifices, and banned Christians from teaching rhetoric and grammar.

An intelligent, humane, and just ruler, Julian was widely popular. If other staunchly pagan emperors had followed him on the throne, Christianity might have been in trouble. His sudden death in 363, however, made him Rome's last pagan emperor. His successors, beginning with Jovian (who also had a short reign), eliminated his anti-Christian policies and Christianity's growth continued apace. Each succeeding year brought hundreds of thousands of new conversions, which endowed the church with greater wealth. Well-to-do converts donated land on which to erect churches and monasteries, and as more churches cropped up, Christian ideas spread to pagans far and wide.

In the midst of this tide of conversion, paganism increasingly came under attack. Christian priests denounced pagan beliefs from the pulpit, and some fanatical Christians persecuted pagans just as pagans had once persecuted them.

Ambrose vs. Symmachus

Nowhere was the growing hostility between Christianity and paganism more pronounced than in Milan. The city's renowned bishop, Ambrose, was ordained in the early 370s. Brilliant, intense, and uncompromising, he influenced a succession of emperors, convincing them that pagan worship should be neither respected nor tolerated.

Ambrose's most famous confrontation with paganism occurred during the rule of Gratian, who reigned in the West from 367 to 383. At the bishop's urging, the emperor stepped down from the office of *pontifex maximus,* chief priest of Rome's traditional state religion. Ambrose was also complicit in Gratian's confiscation of funds belonging to the state priests.

Most controversial of all was Ambrose's demand that the time-honored statue of the pagan goddess Victory be removed from its traditional resting place in Rome's Senate House. Gratian gave the order in 382, shocking and offending Roman pagans everywhere. Two years later, a powerful senator named Quintus Aurelius Symmachus lodged a complaint with Gratian's successor, Valentinian II. Symmachus requested that the statue be restored and with it the spirit of tolerance and understanding. He said,

> The glory of these time makes it suitable that we
> defend the institutions of our ancestors and the rights

and destiny of our country. . . . We demand then the restoration of that condition of religious affairs which was
so long advantageous to the state. . . . We ask then for
peace for the gods of our fathers and of our country. It
is just that all worship should be considered as one. We
look on the same stars, the sky is common, the same
world surrounds us. What difference does it make by
what pains each seeks the truth? We cannot attain to so
great a secret by one road.

THE LOVE OF CUSTOM

In his appeal to the emperor, Symmachus explained what he
saw as the wisdom of following longstanding religious tradition.

*It would at least have been seemly to abstain from injuring
us [and] we beseech you, as old men to leave to posterity what we
received as boys. The love of custom is great. . . . The divine Mind
has distributed different guardians [i.e., deities] and different cults
[faiths] to different cities. As souls are separately given to infants as
they are born, so to peoples the genius of their destiny. . . . Whence
does the knowledge of the gods more rightly come to us, than from
the memory and evidence of prosperity? Now, if a long period gives
authority to religious customs, we ought to keep faith with so many
centuries and follow our ancestors, as they happily followed theirs.*

Ambrose sternly answered the senator's plea by paraphrasing
Symmachus: "Rome complains with sad and tearful words, ask-
ing [for] the restoration of the rites of her ancient ceremonies. . . .

By one road . . . one cannot attain to so great a secret." He then continued with this retort directed at pagans:

> What you [pagans] know not, that we [Christians] know by the voice of God. And what you seek by fancies, we have found out from the very Wisdom and Truth of God. Your ways, therefore, do not agree with ours. . . . You worship the works of your own hands; we think it an offense that anything which can be made should be esteemed God. God wills not that He should be worshipped in stones.

An Astonishing Success

Emperor Valentinian refused Symmachus's petition, and Ambrose went on to launch further attacks on pagan symbols, beliefs, and practices. His influence over Valentinian's co-emperor in the East, Theodosius, was particularly strong.

In 388, for example, some militant Christians in one of Rome's eastern provinces burned down a Jewish synagogue. The emperor condemned the arson and ordered the perpetrators to rebuild the structure. Ambrose intervened and argued that it would not be fitting for Christians to build a Jewish place of worship. Theodosius backed down, the synagogue was never rebuilt, and the criminals remained unpunished. "This was a sad precedent," says Justo González, "for it meant that in an empire calling itself Christian, those whose faith was different would not be protected by the law."

Urged on by Ambrose and other zealous bishops, the government's crusade against paganism continued with renewed vigor. In 391, Theodosius officially closed the remaining pagan temples. Some were torn down, while others became museums or Christian churches. Thereafter, Roman pagans had to worship

St. Peter's Basilica in Rome

in secret. Over time they grew increasingly scarce and finally disappeared from the scene—victims of the transformation of the Roman Empire into a Christian state. Christianity, which would go on to become the spiritual guide for medieval and early modern Europe, "had won against all odds," the noted priest-historian John McManners remarked. "It was an astonishing success story."

Timeline

BCE

ca. 250–68 Period in which modern scholars think the Dead Sea Scrolls were written.

63 Romans enter Palestine and seize Jerusalem.

37–4 Reign of Herod, unpopular Jewish king supported by the Romans.

ca. 7–4 The period in which most modern scholars think Jesus was born.

CE

6 Much of Palestine becomes the Roman province of Judea.

26 Pontius Pilate becomes governor of Judea.

ca. 30–33 Approximate dating of Jesus's crucifixion, ordered by Pontius Pilate.

ca. 36–67 Paul claims to see a vision of the resurrected Jesus and preaches to both Jews and Gentiles.

62	Jesus's brother James is killed in Jerusalem.
64	A devastating fire sweeps through Rome; Emperor Nero blames the Christians.
70	Romans sack Jerusalem during a major Jewish rebellion.
ca. 70–100	The four Gospels of the Bible are compiled.
107	Early Christian bishop Ignatius dies a martyr to the faith.
112	The Roman writer and government official Pliny the Younger consults with the emperor Trajan about how to deal with Christians.
ca. 150	The Apostles' Creed is written in Rome.
193–211	Reign of the emperor Septimius Severus, who launches an anti-Christian persecution.
293	After a long period of social and political unrest, Emperor Diocletian creates a four-man ruling coalition—the Tetrarchy.
303	Diocletian and his co-emperor Galerius launch the worst ever Roman persecution of Christians.

306–337	Rule of Constantine I, who befriends the Christians.
312	After supposedly seeing a cross of light in the sky, Constantine defeats his chief rival at Rome's Milvian Bridge.
313	Constantine and his co-emperor Licinius grant the Christians complete toleration.
324	Constantine becomes sole ruler of the Roman Empire.
325	Bishops at the Council of Nicea, presided over by Constantine, reject the argument of Arius that Jesus was inferior to God.
330	Constantine establishes Constantinople, the first Christian city, on the southern rim of the Black Sea.
337	Constantine accepts Christian baptism on his deathbed.
ca. 337–397	Life of Ambrose, bishop of Milan, who tirelessly fights to suppress pagan beliefs and ceremonies.
354–430	Life of the renowned Christian thinker Augustine, who champions the doctrine of original sin.
363	Death of Julian, the last pagan emperor.

382	Emperor Gratian orders the removal of the statue of the goddess Victory from Rome's Senate House.
384	Symmachus, a nobleman and senator, unsuccessfully petitions to have the statue reinstated.
391	Emperor Theodosius closes the pagan temples.
476	The last Roman emperor is forced to step down from the throne; thereafter, Christianity survives the Empire's demise and becomes the spiritual guide for medieval Europe.

Sources

Chapter One: Greeks, Romans, and Jews
p. 11: "The first Christians were . . ." Justo L. González, *The Story of Christianity, Volume I, The Early Church to the Dawn of the Reformation* (New York: HarperOne, 2010), 7.
p. 12: "in order to understand . . ." Ibid.
pp. 14-15: "The whole world speaks in unison . . ." Aelius Aristides, "Roman Panegyric," in *Roman Civilization, Volume II: The Empire*, eds. Naphtali Lewis and Meyer Reinhold (New York: Columbia University Press, 1990), 23–24, 60.
pp. 15-16: "Hellenism may be defined as . . ." J. R. Porter, *Jesus Christ: The Jesus of History, the Christ of Faith* (New York: Oxford University Press, 2007), 22.
p. 16: "view[ed] Hellenism as . . ." Ibid., 23.
p. 17: "[They] came surging along . . ." Apuleius, *The Golden Ass,* trans. P. G. Walsh (New York: Oxford University Press, 2008), 224.
p. 18: "much of the imagery . . ." Charles Freeman, *Egypt, Greece, and Rome* (New York: Oxford University Press, 2004), 490.
p. 19: "The Pharisees [were Judaism's] spiritual leaders . . ." Michael Grant, *Jesus: An Historian's Review of the Gospels* (New York: Scribner's 1995), 7–8.
p. 20: "The Messiah would come down . . ." A. N. Wilson, *Paul: The Mind of the Apostle* (New York: W. W. Norton, 2000), 7–8.

Chapter Two: Jesus's Life and Teachings
p. 25: "written by members . . ." E. P. Sanders, *The Historical Figure of Jesus* (New York: Penguin, 1996), 49.
p. 25: "Because the Jews at Rome . . ." Suetonius, "Claudius," in *The Twelve Caesars,* trans. Robert Graves, rev. Michael Grant (New York: Penguin, 2003), 202.
pp. 25-26: "There was about this time Jesus . . ." Flavius Josephus, "Antiquities of the Jews," in *The Works of Flavius Josephus, Volume IV*, trans. William Whiston (Grand Rapids, MI: Baker Book House, 1984), 11.
p. 29: "A more plausible theory . . ." Porter, *Jesus Christ*, 37.
p. 30: "In those days came John the Baptist . . ." Matthew 3:1–17 (Revised Standard Version).
pp. 32: "Judge not . . ." Ibid., 7:1.
pp. 32-33: "You have heard . . ." Ibid., 5:38–40.

Chapter Three: The Mission to the Gentiles
p. 36: "When we have looked at the evidence . . ." Wilson, *Paul,* 17–18.
p. 37: "While he felt called to preach . . ." González, *The Story of Christianity,* 27.
p. 37: "They found the stone . . ." Luke 24: 2–3, 37–38, 46–49 (RSV).
p. 39: "the way, and the truth . . . John 14: 6 (RSV).
p. 41: "I persecuted [the] Way to the death . . ." Acts 22: 4–5 (RSV).

p. 42:   "About noon, a great light from heaven . . ." Ibid., 22: 6–10.
p. 42:   "[Jesus said] 'I have appeared to you . . .'" Ibid., 26: 16–18.
p. 44   "The destruction of Jerusalem . . ." Porter, *Jesus Christ*, 173.
p. 45:   "It guaranteed the survival . . ." Wilson, *Paul*, 73.

Chapter Four: Early Organization and Worship
p. 48:   "In AD 100 . . ." Tony Lane, *Exploring Christian Thought* (Nashville: Thomas Nelson, 1996), 8.
p. 49:   "Do you believe in God . . ." "The Apostles' Creed," quoted in González, *The Story of Christianity*, 64.
p. 50:   "You should live in an unblameable unity . . ." Ignatius, "Epistle to the Ephesians, Fourth Letter." http://www.ccel.org/ccel/schaff/anf01.v.ii.iv.html.
p. 51:   "The flow of funds . . ." Brian Moynahan, *The Faith: A History of Christianity* (New York: Doubleday, 2002), 62–63.
p. 52:   "The clergy did not initially wear . . ." Henry Chadwick, "The Early Christian Community," in *The Oxford History of Christianity*, ed. John McManners (Oxford: Oxford University Press, 2002), 37.
p. 55:   "Bishop: God be with you . . ." Moynahan, *The Faith*, 56.
p. 55:   "The [eventual] message to women . . ." Michael D. Coogan, ed., *The Oxford History of the Biblical World* (New York: Oxford University Press, 2001), 553.

Chapter Five: Persecutors and Apologists
p. 60:   "To understand the persecution . . ." Chester G. Starr, *A History of the Ancient World* (New York: Oxford University Press, 1991), 616.
p. 61:   "were popularly charged . . ." Kenneth S. Latourette, *A History of Christianity* (Peabody, MA: Prince, 1999), 82.
p. 61:   "Because they refused . . ." Ibid., 81–82.
p. 62:   "Christians were an ignorant lot . . ." González, *The Story of Christianity*, 50–51.
p. 63:   "[Nero] punished with every refinement . . ." Tacitus, *The Annals of Ancient Rome*, trans. Michael Grant (New York: Penguin, 1989), 365–366.
p. 66:   "These people must not be hunted out . . ." Pliny the Younger, *The Letters of the Younger Pliny*, trans. Betty Radice (New York: Penguin, 1983), 295.
p. 67:   "she finally was placed in a net . . ." Eusebius, *Ecclesiastical History*, in *Readings in European History*, eds. Leon Bernard and Theodore B. Hodges (New York: Macmillan, 1962), 34.
pp. 68-69: "We are held to be criminals . . ." Tertullian, *Apology*, in *Sources of Western Civilization: Rome*, ed. William G. Sinnigen (New York: The Free Press, 1977), 201–202.

Chapter Six: The Faith Finds a Friend

p. 72:   "a simple and joyful message . . ." L. P. Wilkinson, *The Roman Experience* (Lanham, MD: University Press of America, 1975), 196.

p. 72:   "it is certainly likely . . ." Freeman, *Egypt, Greece, and Rome,* 499.

p. 75:   "We saw with our own eyes . . ." Eusebius, "The Church History of Eusebius, Book VIII." http://www.synaxis.org/cf/volume24/ECF00010.htm.

p. 76:   "In his sleep . . ." Eusebius, *Life of Constantine,* in *Sources in Medieval History: The Middle Ages, Volume 1,* ed. Brian Tierney (New York: McGraw-Hill, 1998), 16.

p. 77:   "Constantine knew and cared nothing . . ." A. H. M. Jones, *Constantine and the Conversion of Europe* (Amarillo, TX: Jones Press, 2008), 90.

p. 78:   "the conversion of Constantine . . ." Moynahan, *The Faith,* 89.

p. 79:   "All over the Empire . . ." Charles Freeman, *The World of the Romans* (New York: Oxford University Press, 1993), 162–163.

Chapter Seven: Rethinking Religious Beliefs

p. 82:   "the late fourth and early fifth centuries . . ." Freeman, *Egypt, Greece, and Rome,* 512.

p. 83:   "privilege and position . . ." González, *The Story of Christianity,* 136.

p. 86:   "Jesus had not got . . ." Michael Grant, *Constantine the Great: The Man and His Times* (New York: Scribner's, 1993), 168.

p. 86:   "caused the storm . . ." Ibid.

p. 87:   "We believe in one God . . ." "The Nicene Creed," quoted in Lane, *Exploring Christian Thought,* 28.

p. 88:   "There are three individualities . . ." Ibid., 34.

p. 88:   "Therefore as sin came . . ." Romans 5: 12 (RSV).

p. 88:   "sin dwelleth in [man] . . ." Saint Augustine, *Confessions,* tr. J. G. Pilkington (Edinburgh: T. & T. Clark, 1876), 199.

Chapter Eight: The Transformation of the State

p. 92:   "The collaboration of the state . . ." Freeman, *Egypt, Greece, and Rome,* 517.

p. 93:   "The victories and civil . . ." Edward Gibbon, *The Decline and Fall of the Roman Empire, Volume 1,* ed. David Womersley (New York: Penguin, 1994), 725.

pp. 94-95: "to the future of Christianity . . ." Jones, *Constantine and the Conversion of Europe,* 207.

pp. 96-97: "The glory of these times . . ." Symmachus, quoted in Tierney, *Sources in Medieval History,* 22–23.

p. 97:   "It would at least have been seemly . . ." Ibid., 22.

pp. 97-98: "Rome complains with . . ." Ibid., 23–25.

p. 98:   "This was a sad precedent . . ." González, *The Story of Christianity,* 192.

p. 99:   "had won against all odds . . ." McManners, ed., *The Oxford History of Christianity,* 1.

Bibliography

Selected Books

Cameron, Averil. *The Later Roman Empire: AD 284–430*. Cambridge, MA: Harvard University Press, 2007.

Coogan, Michael D., ed. *The Oxford History of the Biblical World*. New York: Oxford University Press, 2001.

———. *The Old Testament: A Historical and Literary Introduction to the Hebrew Scriptures*. New York: Oxford University Press, 2005.

Crossan, John D. *The Birth of Christianity*. San Francisco: HarperCollins, 1999.

Crossan, John D. and Jonathan L. Reed. *Excavating Jesus*. San Francisco: HarperCollins, 2002.

González, Justo L. *A Concise History of Christian Doctrine*. Nashville: Abingdon, 2006.

———. *The Story of Christianity, Volume I, The Early Church to the Dawn of the Reformation*. New York: HarperOne, 2010.

Grant, Michael. *Constantine the Great: The Man and His Times*. New York: Scribner's, 1993.

———. *Jesus: An Historian's Review of the Gospels*. New York: Scribner's, 1995.

Harris, Roberta L. *The World of the Bible*. New York: Thames and Hudson, 1995.

Jones, A. H. M. *Constantine and the Conversion of Europe*. Amarillo, TX: Jones Press, 2008.

Josephus, Flavius. *The Works of Flavius Josephus, Volume IV*. Translated by William Whiston. Grand Rapids, MI: Baker Book House, 1984.

Lane, Tony. *Exploring Christian Thought*. Nashville: Thomas Nelson, 1996.

Latourette, Kenneth S. *A History of Christianity*. Peabody, MA: Prince, 1999.

MacHaffie, Barbara J. *Her Story: Women in Christian Tradition*. Minneapolis: Augsburg Fortress, 2006.

MacMullen, Ramsay. *Christianizing the Roman Empire, A.D. 100–400*. New Haven: Yale University Press, 1986.

McManners, John, ed. *The Oxford History of Christianity*. Oxford: Oxford University Press, 2002.

Moynahan, Brian. *The Faith: A History of Christianity*. New York: Doubleday, 2002.

Perowne, Stewart. *Caesars and Saints: The Rise of the Christian State, A.D. 180–313*. New York: Barnes and Noble, 2003.

Pilkington, J. G., trans. *The Confessions of Saint Augustine, Bishop of Hippo*. Edinburgh: T. & T. Clark, 1876.

Porter, J. R. *Jesus Christ: The Jesus of History, the Christ of Faith*. New York: Oxford University Press, 1999.

Sanders, E. P. *The Historical Figure of Jesus*. New York: Penguin, 1996.

———. *Jesus and Judaism*. Minneapolis: Fortress, 1993.

Sordi, Marta. *The Christians and the Roman Empire*. Norman: University of Oklahoma Press, 1994.

Wilken, Robert L. *The Christians as the Romans Saw Them*. New Haven: Yale University Press, 2003.

Wilson, A. N. *Paul: The Mind of the Apostle*. New York: W. W. Norton, 2000.

Glossary

apocalyptic: Having to do with the end of the world or Judgment Day.

apology: In ancient times, a document that explained or defended someone's beliefs or actions.

Apostles: Jesus's initial close followers.

baptism: The act of using water to initiate a person into a faith.

basilica: A large Roman building used originally as a law court and later as a model for Christian churches.

begotten: Born.

canon: A collection of religious books; a bible.

creed: A list or statement of beliefs.

deacon: A church official who aids a priest.

doctrine: A religious idea, principle, or policy.

epistle: A letter.

Eucharist: The ceremony or act of Holy Communion, in which a worshiper eats bread and drinks wine.

Gentile: A non-Jew.

Gospels: The first four books of the New Testament: Matthew, Mark, Luke, and John.

Hellenism: Greek culture in ancient times.

heresy: A concept or movement perceived to harm or distort accepted church doctrines or policies.

homoousios: The principle of Jesus and God being equal and of the same substance.

Judaism: The religion of the Jews.

Messiah: A superhuman figure sent by God to save the Jews.

Monastic movement: The spread of monasteries, where monks live a solitary, simple existence.

monotheism: The belief that there is one god.

mystery cult: Ancient faiths that originated in Greece or the Middle East and had secret initiations.

New Testament: Holy books written after Jesus's death that are part of the Christian Bible.

Old Testament: Jewish holy books incorporated into the Christian Bible.

original sin: The idea that humans are born as sinners because of Adam's transgression against God.

pagan: Non-Christian.

polytheism: The belief that there are multiple gods.

pontifex maximus: The chief priest of ancient Rome's state religion, a post traditionally held by the emperors.

presbyter: An early Christian priest.

repent: To admit and apologize for one's guilt.

scriptures: Sacred religious writings.

syncretism: The equation of one god with gods of other faiths.

Trinity: The Christian principle of one God in three persons—Father, Son, and Holy Spirit.

Web sites

From Jesus to Christ: The First Christians
http://www.pbs.org/wgbh/pages/frontline/shows/religion/

Guide to Early Church Documents
http://www.iclnet.org/pub/resources/christian-history.html

Judaism
http://www.religionfacts.com/judaism/index.htm

Early Christian Writings
http://www.earlychristianwritings.com/index.html

Christian Beliefs
http://geneva.rutgers.edu/src/christianity/major.html

Index

Photo Credits

7: Used under license from iStockphoto.com

10-11: Used under license from iStockphoto.com

13: North Wind Picture Archives/Alamy

17: Courtesy of Jeff Dahl

20-21: Private collection

22-23: Art Directors & TRIP / Alamy

28: Archive Images / Alamy

30-31: Archive Images / Alamy

34-35: North Wind Picture Archives / Alamy

38-39: Mary Evans Picture Library / Alamy

46: Classic Image/Alamy

48: Private collection

52-53: Used under license from iStockphoto.com

56-57: Northwind Picture Archives/Alamy

58-59: INTERFOTO/Alamy

64-65: Courtesy Andrei nacu

66: Private collection

68-69: The Art Archive/Alamy

73: Private collection

74-75: Mary Evans Picture Library/Alamy

80: Private collection

84:Private collection

89: Private collection

90-91: Courtesy of jaymce

93: Private collection

94: Private collection

99: Courtesy of Wolfgang Stuck

Book cover and interior design by Derrick Carroll Creative.